BERKELEY IN 90 MINUTES

Berkeley
IN 90 MINUTES

Paul Strathern

IVAN R. DEE
CHICAGO

BERKELEY IN 90 MINUTES. Copyright © 2000 by
Paul Strathern. All rights reserved, including the right to
reproduce this book or portions thereof in any form. For
information, address: Ivan R. Dee, Publisher, 1332 North
Halsted Street, Chicago 60622. Manufactured in the United
States of America and printed on acid-free paper.

Library of Congress Cataloging-in-Publication Data:
Strathern, Paul, 1940–
    Berkeley in 90 minutes / Paul Strathern.
      p. cm.
    Includes bibliographical references and index.
    ISBN 1-56663-290-0 (alk. paper)—ISBN 1-56663-291-9
(pbk. : alk. paper)
    1. Berkeley, George, 1685–1753.   I. Title: Berkeley in
ninety minutes.   II. Title.

B1348 .S75 2000
192—dc21   99-058564

Contents

BERKELEY IN 90 MINUTES

Introduction

Berkeley is the sort of philosopher who gives philosophy a bad name. When you first read his work you think it's ludicrous. And you're right, it is. Berkeley's philosophy denies the existence of matter. According to him, there is no material world.

Modern philosophy had been started in the seventeenth century by the French philosopher René Descartes, who maintained that our only true knowledge of the world is based upon reason. Less than half a century later this Cartesianism, as it was called, was opposed by the English philosopher John Locke, who founded empiricism. Locke took a more commonsense view, claiming that our only true knowledge of the world must be based upon experience.

It was perhaps inevitable that philosophy wouldn't remain constricted within the straitjacket of common sense for long. Just twenty years after Locke's *Essay on Human Understanding* came Berkeley's *Essay Towards a New Theory of Vision*, which set philosophy free from what most of us regard as reality. This carried Locke's empirical thought through to some very noncommonsensical conclusions. According to Berkeley, if our knowledge is based entirely upon experience, we can only know our own experience. We don't in fact know the world, just our particular perceptions of it. So what happens to the world when we are not experiencing it? As far as we are concerned, it simply ceases to exist.

So according to Berkeley, when you don't see something it isn't there. This position is adopted by infants who screw their eyes closed when they wish to avoid eating any more spinach and prune puree. Yet by the time we have achieved the exalted status when we eat our spinach and prunes separately (or not at all), we have usually grown out of this attitude. But not Berkeley. According to him, a tree isn't there if we don't see it or perceive it in any other way, such as touch or smell. So what happens to the tree? Berkeley was a God-fearing man, who eventually became a bishop. This led him to an ingenious explanation as to how the world persists when we don't experience it. His position is simply explained in the following two limericks:

There was a young man who said, "God
Must think it exceedingly odd
     If he finds that this tree
     Continues to be
When there's no one about in the Quad."

And the reply:

Dear Sir:
     Your astonishment's odd:
I am always about in the Quad.
     And that's why this tree
     Will continue to be
Since observed by

Yours faithfully,
GOD.

In other words: we can know that the world exists only when we are perceiving it. Yet even when we are not directly perceiving the world, it is nonetheless supported by the continuous perception of an all-seeing God.

Berkeley's empirical conclusion (no permanent reality) and his miraculous solution (an ever-present God) sounds like so much sophistry. Today's sensibilities for the most part have little time for such apparent intellectual trickery—which seems to belong more to the Middle Ages than to our age of science. So it comes as some surprise when we find that subatomic physics has been forced to a surprisingly similar conclusion to Berkeley's. According to Heisenberg's uncertainty principle, we cannot simultaneously measure both the momentum and position of a subatomic particle. If one of these elements is measured (i.e., perceived), the other remains indeterminate. Thus, in a very real sense, only the quality which is being perceived (the measured position, say) is real, and the other quality (its momentum: mass and velocity) does not exist in any determinable form. We can only "know" the one we are perceiving. The other element is in a sense "there" (as if perceived by an all-seeing God), but it cannot come into any determinate existence until we perceive it.

Berkeley's philosophy appeared to take empiricism to a ludicrous extreme. But when we follow through the implications of our commonsense assumptions to their logical conclusions, the result often has little to do with the "obvious" commonsense assumptions from which we started. Common sense is how we attempt to run our everyday lives. But if we wish to progress beyond the imprecision and muddle of everyday existence to some more certain truth, we frequently have to abandon the obvious. As Einstein remarked: "Common sense is the collection of prejudices acquired by age eighteen."

Berkeley's Life and Works

Berkeley was the first (and last) Irishman to make a major contribution to philosophy. He was born on March 12, 1685, in the county town of Kilkenny, sixty miles southwest of Dublin. His father was a royalist English immigrant who referred to himself as a gentleman, but was in fact a young officer in the dragoons who became a farmer.

George Berkeley was brought up near Kilkenny in a stone farmhouse on the banks of the River Nore, beside the ruined tower of Dysert Castle. The farmhouse may originally have been one of the castle's outbuildings, and it too is now a ruin. The last time I visited this spot, all that remained of Berkeley's house was some low tumbledown walls overgrown with vines. Across the field was the ruined tower of Dysert Castle with crows cawing about the battlements. Beneath the wooded hills the setting sun glinted in the curve of the river. It must have been much the same in Berkeley's day.

When Berkeley was eleven he was sent away to board at Kilkenny College, the best school in Ireland at the time. Both the satirist Jonathan Swift and the playwright William Congreve had been educated there during the previous decade. At the age of fifteen Berkeley went on to Trinity College, Dublin, which had been founded two hundred years earlier by Elizabeth I to educate one of her ignorant young admirers.

In 1704, at the age of nineteen, Berkeley received his B.A. degree. He had obviously enjoyed himself as an undergraduate, because he hung around in Dublin for the next few years "waiting to take up a fellowship." During this period Berkeley started to read Locke and the French philosopher Malebranche, the leading exponent of Cartesianism. Berkeley agreed with Locke's empirical belief that all knowledge comes from the senses, but he realized that this resulted in a materialism which didn't leave much room for God. Throughout Berkeley's life he remained a sincerely religious man and firmly resisted any tendency toward atheism. But how could he maintain his empiricism while retaining his belief in God?

Ingeniously Berkeley showed how Locke's belief in materialism was mistaken. He pointed out that we may derive our knowledge from our experience, but this consists only of sensations. We have no access to any underlying material substance which might give rise to these sensations. Despite its apparent absurdity, this argument is profound. It led Berkeley to his famous conclusion: *esse est percipi* (to be is to be perceived). This triumphantly overcame materialism, but it left Berkeley with the problem of what happened to the world when no one was looking. As we have seen, Berkeley suggested that God is always looking. He derived this view from Malebranche, who held that change is not caused by objects interacting in cause and effect, but by the continuous action of God upon the world.

Berkeley put forward his ideas in *An Essay Towards a New Theory of Vision*, which he published in 1709, and *A Treatise Concerning the Principles of Human Knowledge*, published in 1710. These works, which pulled a lot more than the rug from under the feet of earlier philosophers, caused a sensation. But they are difficult to understand unless you have the staying power of a philosophical steeplechaser. Many readers don't last beyond the first fence, with an opening sentence such as: "It is evident to any one who takes a survey of the objects of human knowledge, that they are either *ideas* actually (1) imprinted on the senses, or else such as are (2) perceived by attending to the passions and operations of the mind, or lastly, ideas (3) formed by help of memory and imagination, either compounding, dividing, or barely representing those originally perceived in the aforesaid ways."

Fortunately Berkeley also put forward his ideas in *Three Dialogues Between Hylas and Philonous*. These are much more amenable, and begin with Philonous coming across the insomniac Hylas beneath a "purple sky" at dawn with the "wild but sweet notes of birds" twittering around them. These dialogues clarify Berkeley's ideas, which as we have seen started with common sense and then moved, quite reasonably, to the unreasonable. There is no reason why philosophy should conform to common sense (indeed, there are only brief periods when philosophy has had much to do with it), but people appeared to expect otherwise. Berkeley soon became an object of public ridicule, and as a result was stoutly defended by all anti-philistine intellectuals.

Not surprisingly, many of Berkeley's contemporaries didn't consider him to be an empiricist at all. Instead they saw him as an out-and-out metaphysician. There is some truth in this, despite Berkeley's insistence to the contrary. Berkeley's empiricism reduces him to a solipsist: one who believes that he alone exists in the world. After all, if my experience is the only reality, how can I possibly know that anyone else exists? All I experience when I see someone else is a collection of impressions. From this, common sense may lead me to infer that this other person exists in very much the same manner as I do. But I do not actually experience this. It is a supposition which is not based upon any perception of mine.

Similarly, Berkeley's idea that the world itself was maintained by the continuous perception of an all-seeing God is certainly not supported by experience. It is metaphysical: that is, it goes beyond any physical knowledge we are capable of discovering. This leaves Berkeley in the curious position of being both a thoroughgoing empiricist and a thoroughgoing metaphysician—an apparent self-contradiction. Yet this self-contradiction lies at the very heart of our present worldview. Most modern philosophy, and all scientific thought, finds itself in a similar position. Before we can proceed to a rational or scientific explanation of the world, we must first make several far-reaching assumptions that are not derived from experience, and are thus metaphysical presuppositions. For instance, we assume that the world is consistent. From this we go on to assume that it conforms to the laws of logic as we conceive them. Likewise this leads us to believe that this reality in some extremely precise and intimate way conforms to mathematics. A similarly important assumption we make is that the world somehow "matches" our perception. What possible experience could we have that would reveal to us that our perceptions have anything whatsoever to do with what gives rise to them? (A blindfolded patient experiences an extremely sharp localized pain. This could be caused by a needle, an electrode, a bee sting, a drop of concentrated acid, and so on. Which is it? Which of these does his pain *resemble*? It doesn't of course *resemble* any of them. It only resembles similar sensations, not whatever might have caused them.)

Other "obvious" assumptions we make about our experience are equally unwarranted. Take one of the basic laws of logic, that of identity. This basically states that a thing is itself, and everything else is not that thing. A thing cannot be itself and also something else at the same time. We disobey this law every time we confront a work of art. A painting of a landscape, for instance, is viewed simultaneously as a landscape and as a piece of canvas daubed with colored pigments. It may be argued that what we gain from aesthetic perception is not really knowledge. Even so, it remains an important component of the way we perceive the world. Every time we look at a picture, an image on a screen, or even words on a page, it involves a similar process. This is a central part of our experience, and it contradicts the laws of logic.

There is yet more damaging evidence against our all-but-unconscious precognitive assumptions concerning logical consistency and such. Even science itself must accommodate illogicality. The law of identity doesn't break down only in aesthetic perception. Something surprisingly similar also takes place in modern quantum physics—which states that light can be viewed as either waves or particles. This defies logical consistency (a wave is simply a motion; a particle is an object). It has been argued that such exceptions simply serve to reinforce the general rule, where logical consistency is concerned. Whether or not this is the case, they certainly reinforce the notion that logical consistency is a metaphysical assumption—and, as such, no more (or less) supportable than Berkeley's idea that the world is supported by the continuous perception of an all-seeing God.

Interestingly, this latter idea (or its equivalent) has a long pedigree in mathematics. The early Arab mathematicians, who advanced this field of learning almost single-handedly during the period between the decline of the Hellenistic world and the Renaissance, developed their own mathematical philosophy. This provided them with an intellectual and spiritual justification of mathematics. According to their philosophy, mathematics was the way God's mind worked. And since God made the world, it was bound to work according to mathematics. By learning more about mathematics, they were learning more about the mind of God. This was both a profound and a beautiful idea—and as such it even resembled mathematics itself!

It is not difficult to discern the shadow of this metaphysical idea behind Berkeley's idea of a world supported by God's perception. If anything, this Arabic notion of mathematics actually informs Berkeley's idea. How does God's all-seeing continuous perception actually see the world? Why, in a way such that the world obeys the laws of his thought: that is, the laws of mathematics and science (or nature). Such laws *are* God's perception. The Arab notion of mathematics was of course rooted in Islamic theology, but this didn't prevent its adoption by Christianity. Indeed, it persisted long after Arab mathematics had been superseded by the European tradition, which was developed after the Renaissance by the likes of Descartes, Pascal, and Fermat. Berkeley's eighteenth-century contemporary, Isaac Newton, certainly believed in it.

Only with the complete divorce of theology and science was this idea replaced. Modern mathematical philosophy dispenses with the idea of God, which leaves it in a curious situation. Without God, where does mathematics exist? And how does it exist? Is it simply our way of seeing the world? In other words, could there be another form of mathematics for beings equipped with a different perceptual apparatus? When a mathematician produces a new theory, has he discovered it or has he created it? Did it come into being for the first time in his head, or was it always there, somewhere, waiting to be discovered? In other words, would $2 + 2 = 4$ be true if there was no one (even God) to think it? Extend that $2 + 2 = 4$ to the "laws of nature" and the enormity of the problem becomes apparent. These are the ultimate problems of reality. Berkeley's solution to this problem may seem fanciful and far-fetched, but it at least answers these questions. Contemporary mathematical and scientific philosophers still find themselves in a quandary over this matter. Stephen Hawking even ends his *Brief History of Time* by claiming that "if we discover a complete theory" (i.e., of everything) this could lead us to "know the mind of God." Without a metaphysical philosophy (such as Berkeley's) to back them up, such idle statements by scientists must remain empty of any meaning.

Given Berkeley's anti-materialist stance, it

may seem odd that he should write a work entitled *An Essay Towards a New Theory of Vision*. Surely the entire notion of vision is intimately linked with the scientific, materialist view of the world? There are two main reasons for Berkeley's emphasis on this subject. First, the recent invention of the microscope and the telescope had caused a revolution in the whole idea of "vision." Using his telescope, Galileo had been the first to see the rings of Saturn. Hooke, gazing down his microscope, was the first to see what he named "cells" in a living organism. Any new philosophy had to take into account this expansion into the micro- and macro-world. (According to medieval philosophy, everything in the world had been created by God for a purpose. But it was difficult to conceive how such things as cells and the rings of Saturn had a purpose, when they had remained unknown and unseen since the beginning of time.)

Yet Berkeley had an even more pressing need to address the problem of vision. It is our sight that most convinces us of the existence of the world around us. As soon as we open our eyes, we see it. Of course the world exists; our common sense (prompted by our eyes) tells us so.

Berkeley attacks this problem head on, so to speak. And his precise empirical analysis of our perceptual situation is both masterly and (almost) convincing. When we perceive—when we see, touch, smell, and so forth—what happens? There are just two entities taking part in this process, and no more. There is the perceiving subject, and there is what it perceives. The latter consists, for us, of color, shape, smell, and so forth. There is no such thing as some existing matter *beyond* what we perceive. What we perceive has no "absolute existence" beyond our perception of it. Its being is our perception. *Esse est percipi* (to be is to be perceived). There is no such thing as matter, only perception.

We may find it difficult (or in practice impossible) to conduct our everyday existence on this level. Yet Berkeley's argument is all but impossible to refute. His biographer, A. A. Luce, went so far as to claim that this immaterialist position adopted by Berkeley "has never been answered except by misrepresentation and ridicule." Most of us choose not to assume Berkeley's ridiculous position, and prefer to rely upon the misrepresentation of our common sense. But if we are scrupulous and rigid in our search for philosophical truth, we may arrive at a similar position to that maintained by Berkeley.

Meanwhile Berkeley had become a fellow of Trinity College, and in 1710 he was ordained as a Church of Ireland (Protestant) clergyman. Three years later he decided to try his luck in London. By now his books had made him famous, and the Irishman who believed there was no such thing as matter became the flavor-of-the-month during the London social season. He was presented at court by Jonathan Swift; drank burgundy and champagne in the author's box at the opening night of Addison's drama *Cato*; and found that his native Irish wit was more than a match for the fashionable fops and intellectuals of the coffeehouses. According to the poet Alexander Pope, no soft touch in matters of character assessment, Berkeley was possessed of "ev'ry virtue under heav'n."

26

All this sounds a bit too good to be true, but there's no evidence to contradict it in the surprisingly dull definitive biography by A. A. Luce. (During my undergraduate years at Trinity College, Dublin, I attended lectures by the Rev. Luce, who was by then a sprightly and combative septuagenarian. He stoutly adhered to Berkeley's anti-materialist philosophy. Those among us who perversely protested that there might be such a thing as the real world were contemptuously dismissed as "materialists.")

Luce's biography, which despite its author's philosophical stance includes a wealth of material, never quite captures Berkeley's character. In fact, there's very little from any reliable source to indicate what Berkeley was actually like as a person. He doesn't seem to have got himself into anecdotal situations. There's no doubting his fierce intelligence (which he'd have needed to defend his philosophy), and all who met him appear to have been entranced by him. The portraits give him an air of bewigged portly anonymity, and his strongest prevailing characteristic appears to have been a detestation of freethinkers—an almost universal aberration of the period. Otherwise Berkeley seems to have been decent, self-effacing (despite his society fame), yet able to stand up for himself, and invariably motivated by the highest principles. His only flaw seems to have been his philosophy. As his contemporary, the Irish dramatist Oliver Goldsmith, claimed, Berkeley was "the greatest genius or the greatest dunce.... Those slightly acquainted with him thought him a fool," whereas he was "a prodigy of learning and good nature to those who shared his intimate friendship." Here the man and his philosophy appear to be one. As we have seen, there is a lot more to Berkeley's philosophy than is immediately perceived, even if he would be the first to argue otherwise!

Berkeley's most pressing concern at this point in his life was the need for a job. Fortunately his well-connected friend Jonathan Swift eventually managed to fix him up with a post as chaplain to the Earl of Peterborough, who was setting off to become ambassador to the King of Sicily. Berkeley accompanied the earl abroad, and on his way through Paris took the opportunity to call on Malebranche, the disciple of Descartes who had so inspired him. (Most sources agree that this meeting took place on Berkeley's first trip abroad; but A. A. Luce, in his steadfast resolve to render Berkeley's life even more colorless, argues that it didn't take place at all. I am convinced that it took place, and at this juncture in Berkeley's life.)

Malebranche was a priest, and at the time of Berkeley's visit was suffering from a severe inflammation of the lungs. According to Berkeley's early biographer Stock, Malebranche was in his cell brewing some medicine when Berkeley arrived. They began talking together about Berkeley's astonishing new theory, which had just been translated into French. But in Stock's words: "the issue of the debate proved tragical to poor Malebranche. In the heat of disputation he raised his voice so high, and gave way so freely to the natural impetuosity of a man of parts and a Frenchman, that he brought on himself a violent increase of his disorder, which carried him off a few days later."

Fortunately for philosophy, Berkeley had no chance to meet other leading philosophers—and continued with the Earl of Peterborough as far as Leghorn. Here it was discovered that the ambassador's coach and ceremonial regalia had not arrived by boat, and he refused to proceed and take up his appointment until properly equipped. After waiting around for a few months with his sulking employer, Berkeley was released and made his way back to London. He returned just in time for the abortive Jacobite Rebellion of 1715, a Catholic uprising in Scotland which sought to reinstate James II, who in 1714 had been deposed.

A year after his return to England, Berkeley managed to obtain a position as traveling companion to a young invalid named George Ashe, the son of an Irish bishop, who was planning a grand tour of Europe. "Unlimited letters of credit" were provided, and off the two of them went on a tour which was to last four years. Their stagecoach was attacked by a wolf near Grenoble (Berkeley drew his sword, Ashe fired his pistol, and the wolf "very calmly retired, looking back ever and anon"). They crossed the Alps in a snowstorm; and Berkeley fell asleep through a succession of concerts in Rome. They then set off around Italy, which in those days was a kind of cultural theme park and Disneyworld for the idle rich of northern Europe. Such travelers tended to regard the locals much as we regard Mickey Mouse and Donald Duck, but made a habit of going into raptures when they saw the art and architecture produced by these cartoon characters. At Ischia, Berkeley entered into the swing of things with a little Irish exaggeration, claiming that from the top of the island "you have the finest prospect in the world, surveying at one view a tract of Italy 300 miles in length."

In 1720 Berkeley returned to England and within a year published *De Motu* (About Motion). In this book he makes some important scientific pronouncements, rejecting Newton's ideas on absolute space, motion, and time. Berkeley's views uncannily match the findings of modern physics. It's difficult to gauge quite how much he was aware of what he was saying here. Some hold that he was correct, but for utterly the wrong reasons; others that he was the "precursor of Mach and Einstein." But as far as I can gather, Berkeley was chiefly interested in defending his philosophical position rather than mapping out a theory of relativity two hundred years ahead of its time.

The big event of 1720 in London was the South Sea Bubble, the City's first great financial fiasco. The South Sea Company had originally been founded to trade in slaves for South America. By various machinations, based on the minimum of substance, the company's stock began to rise sharply. Investors from far and wide clamored to buy, and the price soared. Inevitably the bubble burst, and a wide range of investors, large and small, were ruined. In the subsequent inquiry the usual round of government ministers, establishment figures, and financial whiz kids were found to have been involved in the fraud. (Those who remain innocent of how these things work will be astonished to learn that the South Sea Company went on trading for well over a century, until 1853, by which time the work of the abolitionist William Wilberforce had long put an end to the company's ostensible raison d'être.)

This unedifying episode had a profound effect on decent men like Berkeley. He published *An Essay Towards Preventing the Ruin of Great Britain* and a long prophetic verse entitled "Westward the Course of Empire Takes Its Way." (As a result of this title, which became a popular saying among the early American pioneers who emigrated to the West Coast, the town of Berkeley in California was named after the philosopher.)

Berkeley now became convinced that the future of civilization no longer lay in perilous Britain and in Europe but in America. He decided to emigrate, and proposed a scheme for building a college in Bermuda. Here "in the Summer Islands" he would educate the sons of planters and native American Indians. In the aftermath of the South Sea Bubble, this high-minded scheme caught the public imagination. Subscriptions poured in, the Archbishop of Canterbury became a trustee, and Parliament voted a grant of twenty thousand pounds sterling.

At the same time, Berkeley also received a bequest of three thousand pounds from the will of a woman named Hester van Homrigh, whom he'd hardly known. This was the famous "Vanessa" who had fallen in love with Berkeley's friend Swift. As is expected of intellectual clergymen, Jonathan Swift's love life was something of a fiasco. He had secretly married his half-sister (or niece) Stella, but had an affair with Vanessa (who was already married) in London. Much to his horror, Vanessa followed him when he returned to Dublin, where he was dean of St. Patrick's Cathedral. She finally had a child by him, which was probably looked after by Stella (the details are suitably obscure and disputed). Vanessa seemingly turned against Swift before she died, and in a fit of pique changed her will in favor of Berkeley.

No one really knows why Berkeley was chosen. He claimed that he had "never in the whole course of my life exchanged a word with her"— which was a fib, because he had been introduced to her by Swift and had been to dinner at her house a few times afterward. But there's no suggestion that Berkeley had a fling with her: he wasn't that sort of person at all. So the mystery remains. Fortunately Berkeley's relationship with Swift survived this episode, and Berkeley is even said to have burned a number of compromising letters between Vanessa and Swift which came his way as a result of the bequest. Berkeley viewed the whole affair as an act of Providence, to assist his Bermuda scheme.

Berkeley and Swift remained friends. They may have been separated by eighteen years of age and a complete disparity of temperaments, but both maintained exceptionally wide-ranging intellectual interests. They didn't always agree, but each recognized in the other a mind of sufficient caliber to test his own ideas. Ironically, though, Berkeley's philosophical position on ideas as such was distinctly skeptical. "Whether others have this wonderful faculty of *abstracting their ideas*, they can best tell: for my self I find indeed I have a faculty of imagining, or representing to my self the ideas of those particular things I have perceived and of variously compounding and dividing them." He goes on to explain how he can imagine a man with two heads, or a centaur. But its parts, such as the ears or eyes, will always be particular in shape and color. "Likewise the idea of man that I frame to my self, must be either of a white, or black, or a tawny, a straight, or a crooked, a tall, or a low, or a middle-sized man." The image he imagines will always be precisely particular with regard to its perceptible qualities. "I cannot by any effort of thought conceive the abstract idea."

This is typical of Berkeley's particular and personal method of arguing. It is rigidly empiricist. He argues from his own experience, and that alone. And in this case it has led critics to suggest an uncommon irregularity in Berkeley's personal perceptual apparatus. They argue that it is not usual to experience things in this fashion, that we all can form an abstract idea of a man, an apple, a centaur, and so forth. But can we? It is possible to summon up a vague, momentary, generalized idea of an apple. But the more closely we examine this idea, the more it takes on particular features—color, size, and so forth. This argument, however, would appear to fail on one important count—with regard to our idea of number. Here our ideas are undeniably abstract, and remain so. Our idea of four does not take on any more particularity the more we think about it.

Think of 4 x 10. During the mental operation that gives you the answer to this sum, did you particularize your number four as 4 or 4? Most people either cannot answer this question or think it irrelevant: their conception of "four" is an abstract idea, not a representation of a numeral. Here, I suggest, even Berkeley would have abstracted his idea, using a mental facility that he claimed not to possess. It is difficult to understand how Berkeley could have made this mistake, for as we shall see he was an excellent mathematician.

To be fair, Berkeley had an answer to such objections. In line with his overall philosophical position, he simply argued that numbers don't exist. This is indeed an original stance for a mathematician to take, but there is no denying that Berkeley maintained it. As we have seen in our earlier discussion of Arab mathematics and the mind of God, the philosophical status of mathematics has long been a matter of profound debate. And many philosophers have come to many different conclusions on this matter. But the question would seem to be *how* mathematics exists, rather than *whether* it exists. Only Berkeley appears to question the latter.

Around this time Berkeley was a frequent visitor to court, where the Princess of Wales held a regular philosophical salon. She had met Leibniz and was keen on talking about philosophy; yet she appears to have talked a lot of nonsense at her salons, and Berkeley was bored to tears. Still, his diplomatic socializing was soon to achieve its purpose. In 1724 he was appointed Dean of Derry, a fairly well-paid post, which he took up while waiting for the details of his Bermuda project to be completed.

During this period Berkeley met Anne Forster, the daughter of the speaker of the Irish Parliament. She had been educated in France and is characterized by most sources as "talented" and "cheerful." No mention is made of them falling in love, but they obviously became friends and in 1728 were married. In the sporting parlance of those times, it was a good match. By now, many of the details of the Bermuda project (except the payment of the vital government grant) had been sorted out, so Berkeley set sail with his new wife for America.

The couple settled in Rhode Island, where Berkeley bought one hundred acres of cleared land (at ten pounds an acre) with the idea of turning this into a farm to support the college in Bermuda. He also built himself a house, which he called Whitehall (after what was then the royal palace in London). This house was described by a contemporary source as "an indifferent wooden house," which it certainly isn't. Drive three miles north from Newport, Rhode Island, and you can still see it on the outskirts of Middleton. It's a plain but substantial two-story, wood-frame farmhouse, its doorway embellished with a neoclassical pediment.

According to reliable local sources, Berkeley was in the habit of walking down to nearby Sachuest Beach, where he would write in the shelter of Hanging Rocks. He also preached regularly at Trinity Church in Newport, which had been built just a couple of years before he arrived and was modeled on the churches that Christopher Wren had recently built in London. This attractive white-painted church still stands, and its spired tower is a local landmark. Inside is an organ with the inscription "The Gift of Dr. George Berkeley late Lord Bishop of Cloyne." Berkeley's infant daughter, who died during this period, is buried in the churchyard.

According to the census taken during Berkeley's time in Newport, the population consisted of "3,843 Whites, 949 Negroes and 248 Indians." Newport was then one of the most thriving towns in America. The big money came from shipping—the ships making the triangular trip to Africa to pick up slaves, then crossing to the West Indian plantations, where they sold the slaves and brought home molasses, rum, and gold doubloons. Berkeley was repelled by the slave trade but made no remarks about it during his stay. It is possible he didn't realize how deeply the town was implicated in this business. He also took no part in any of the religious disputes that sometimes arose between the local Baptists, Quakers, and Presbyterians, who apparently all flocked to hear him preach.

For the most part, Berkeley's trip to America was a waste of time. After waiting for three years he learned that the government had decided not to give him a grant after all. (Instead the money was diverted to more pressing needs and given to the Princess Royal for her dowry.) Berkeley returned to Britain, where he once again became a regular at court. The Princess of Wales had now become queen and wanted to hear all about his marvelous time in America. Meanwhile Berkeley continued with his attacks on freethinkers, issuing *The Analyst: or, a Discourse Addressed to an Infidel Mathematician.*

The "infidel mathematician" in question was Edmund Halley, after whom the comet is named. Halley was one of the leading scientific minds of his day. He had not only been the first to calculate the orbit of a comet but was also sufficiently expert to have corrected the proofs of Newton's *Principia.* As far as I can discover, Halley's only gaffe was his attempt to found meteorology as a serious science. But in Berkeley's view he had done far worse by expressing the opinion that "the doctrines of Christianity are incomprehensible, and religion itself an imposture." This was too much for Berkeley, whose main thesis in *Discourse* was that religion was no more incomprehensible than mathematics. According to Berkeley, both mathematics and religion rested on foundations that remained equally beyond our comprehension. Indeed, Berkeley went one step further. In line with his contention that numbers don't exist, he set about attempting to *disprove* mathematics. The fact that he made use of mathematics to do this does not seem to have bothered him a bit.

Despite such seeming absurdities, Berkeley's argument remains of deep philosophical significance. Indeed, his paper has been hailed by the mathematicial historian Florian Cajori as "the most spectacular event of the century in the history of British mathematics." Since the eighteenth century also witnessed the mathematics of Newton, one can only assume that Cajori believed Berkeley succeeded in his disproof. To have advanced mathematics with such consummate skill as Newton, one of the greatest mathematical geniuses of all time, was one thing. To have put an end to the entire enterprise would certainly have been the most spectacular mathematical event of the century.

Berkeley's main attack on mathematics centers on the notion of the infinite. According to mathematics, a line of finite length can be subdivided into an infinite number of infinitely small segments. (Calculus, which had recently been discovered by Newton and Leibniz, is based upon this principle.) Berkeley argued that the idea of an infinitely divisible line of finite length was self-contradictory. The division of the line must continue indefinitely (for it to consist of infinitely small segments), yet at the same time it must also abruptly stop (because the line comes to an end). You cannot have it both ways.

Likewise, Berkeley argued that if a finite line consists of infinitely small parts, these parts must at some stage take on finite length. At what point do these infinitely small segments "grow" into segments of finite length? As soon as they make up a finite segment of the whole, be it ever so small, this segment too is infinitely divisible. So do they only become finite when they make up the entire finite line? But what if the line were a bit shorter? Such questions can continue ad infinitum. . . .

Berkeley's answer is both simple and logical. There is no such thing as infinite divisibility. So, according to the laws of logic, divisibility is therefore finite. This means that we must end up with distinct "atoms" of length. Berkeley was aware that such thinking led to some odd conclusions. For instance, Euclid's geometrical method of dividing a line in two equal segments was invalidated. Why? Such a thing was impossible if the line consisted of an odd number of indivisible length-atoms.

Berkeley's objections to mathematics in fact proved irrefutable. He had, after his own fashion, "disproved" mathematics. Being a mathematician of some ability, he was willing to concede that mathematics certainly "worked."

44

But he had just as certainly proved his point: mathematics was based upon mysteries that were as unfathomable as those of religion. As it happened, Berkeley's "disproof" of mathematics was to prove unanswerable for well over a century. Not until the discovery of non-Euclidian geometry was it realized that mathematical space and actual space were two entirely different entities. Infinite divisibility was quite possible in mathematical space, even if in reality such a thing was impossible.

As we have already seen, Berkeley also launched a bold philosophical attack on science in *De Motu*. This was equally ahead of its time and equally consistent with his own essentially unscientific philosophy. Newton's theory of universal gravity included the notions of absolute motion and absolute space. In other words, a quantity of space, such as a certain length, could be measured against an absolute unchanging scale. The same applied to a quantity of time. Both entities were utterly fixed!

Berkeley suggested that there could be no such thing as absolute motion: it must always be relative, and must always involve physical entities. Motion was the way the world was perceived by the "Author of Nature." In the course of such arguments this was the phrase that Berkeley frequently used for God. To equate the "Author of Nature" with the "laws of nature" makes Berkeley's philosophy much more palatable and comprehensible to the modern sensibility. But Berkeley himself would certainly not have accepted the identity of these two concepts.

So motion was not absolute, it could not be separated from the world. Likewise with absolute space. This was simply an abstract idea—which, unlike the so-called abstract idea of an apple, we cannot clothe with particulars. How big is this absolute space? What does it look like? How can we possibly perceive it? Space too was relative and part of the world: it too was the way the Author of Nature perceived the world. Berkeley's ideas on such matters were largely ignored by scientists until the early twentieth century. Einstein's theory of relativity views space and motion much as they were conceived by

Berkeley, though without Berkeley's immaterialist assumptions.

As a result of enduring long hours of boredom at the royal court, Berkeley was eventually favored with an appointment. He was made Bishop of Cloyne, a diocese in southwest Ireland. This historic bishopric had been founded in the sixth century by St. Colman, who had resigned from the church in disgust because he reckoned they'd got the date of Easter wrong. Now once again Cloyne would have a bishop who believed the rest of the world had the wrong time.

Berkeley and his family (which now included several children) set off across the sea to Dublin and then traveled on the long journey southwest, across the Knockmealdown Mountains, to the remote small town of Cloyne. Here Berkeley was to live for the next eighteen years (1734–1752) in the Seehouse. (The building in which he lived burned down in 1870, but the present large, plain Seehouse is said to be very similar.) His six children grew up, his wife ran the farm (which employed more than a hundred hands), and the family became the focus of local social life—as well as the charity center during hard winters and when the potato crop failed.

It should be remembered that Berkeley was a Protestant and a member of the Anglo-Irish ascendancy. The majority Catholic population lived in subjugation and often extreme poverty. They were victims of English racial prejudice and the fear that any Catholic invasion from Europe would use Ireland as the back door to Britain. Berkeley, with his friend Swift and many other right-thinking Anglo-Irishmen, was appalled at the treatment of the Irish peasantry, which frequently led to widespread starvation. Swift, in his pamphlet *A Modest Proposal*, suggested a solution to this problem: there was no need for hunger in Ireland, because the Irish could easily feed themselves if they ate their own children. But even such bitter sarcasm failed to rouse popular opinion in Britain.

(A Marxist interpretation of Berkeley's thought claims that his entire philosophy is a reflection of this political situation. When you don't see a thing, it isn't there. Ignore the poor, and they don't exist. As with many such interpretations, this is highly ingenious, a potential provider of countless intriguing insights—political, psychological, and philosophical—and utterly bogus. It disingenuously ignores Berkeley's persistent campaigning over the plight of the Irish. Such ideas are art rather than interpretation.)

Berkeley's interest in social matters went far beyond campaigning. His practical knowledge of Irish affairs led him to speculate on methods for remedying the plight of his country. These formed the basis of *The Querist*, published in 1737. At the time, economic thinking was still in its infancy. Adam Smith's *The Wealth of Nations*, which is generally recognized as the founding work of classical economics, would not be published until 1776, nearly forty years later. Nevertheless some of Berkeley's ideas show a profound and imaginative understanding of how commerce worked and how prosperity could best be promoted. Here Berkeley's thinking can be said to concur with Marx's famous maxim, "Philosophers have only interpreted the world in various ways; the point is to change it." Of course Berkeley was certainly no precursor of Marxism; and, as we have seen, the main thrust of his philosophy was very much devoted to interpreting the world.

The Querist takes the form of six hundred "queries," each intended to be of a penetrating or rhetorical nature. Berkeley was among the first to recognize that gold is no real measure of wealth, either on a national or a personal scale. The real virtue of gold is the use to which it can be put. One query asks rhetorically: "Whether there be any virtue in gold or silver, other than as they set people at work, or create industry?" A nation's wealth lay in its labor, in the industry of its citizens. Berkeley asks tellingly: "Whether there ever was, is, or will be, an industrious nation poor or an idle one rich?" In Berkeley's view, Ireland's problems stemmed to a large extent from the laziness and backwardness of its indigenous population—though he recognized that this was hardly their own fault. Ireland suffered because a large proportion of its land was owned by absentee landlords living in England, who saw their estates merely as a source of income. The neglect of these estates led to a poverty-stricken and dispirited population. As a corollary, the country also suffered from excessive exports at the expense of useful imports, which might have helped to generate commerce. Christian compassion and personal inclination led Berkeley to one fundamental conclusion. The welfare of those with the least should be the aim of all economic policy. He asked: "Whether a people can be called poor, where the common sort are well fed, clothed and lodged?" Poverty and starvation, the scourge of Ireland, could be eliminated.

Berkeley also recognized the importance of banks in generating trade. It was "the greatest spur to commerce that property can be so readily conveyed and so well secured by a *comte en banc* [bank account], that is, by only writing one man's name for another's in a bank book." Central banks had already been successfully established in Amsterdam, London, and Hamburg, though the idea had not worked in France— where the first national bank had collapsed, causing a financial disaster even greater than the South Sea Bubble (which burst in the same year). The Bank of England, on the other hand, had proved sufficiently resilient to weather the South Sea Bubble. Berkeley advocated the establishment of a National Bank in Ireland.

Berkeley's economic and financial philosophy raised a great deal of interest. There were no less than ten editions of *The Querist* published during his lifetime, and Adam Smith was almost certainly influenced by some of his ideas. But Berkeley's stress on Ireland and its particular situation meant that his ideas did not achieve such widespread influence as many economic theories less rooted in reality. Despite this his ideas were farsighted. During the grim years of World War II, when neutral Ireland was isolated and poverty-stricken, a vain attempt was even made to revive the economy by applying some of his ideas.

In later life Berkeley became interested in art. Among the paintings in the Seehouse was a Van Dyck, and among the members of the household are listed a music master and an artist-tutor. The bishop seems to have run a large and rather varied dwelling. A local "patriot" came to stay and never left; two clergymen took up residence; and there appear to have been a number of "aunts," to say nothing of servants, half a dozen children, several dogs of diminishing pedigree and obedience, a beribboned pet lamb, and a donkey. On the one occasion when the family went for a holiday in Killarney, the bishop's main party required fourteen beds (not including accommodations for servants and grooms).

Meanwhile Berkeley himself went quietly to seed. He was now in his fifties and looking decidedly middle-aged. According to most sources, he lived "a sendentary life"—took practically no exercise, grew fat, and suffered increasing respiratory and circulatory problems as well as bouts of "nervous cholic." He also became a little dotty. Some claim that this mild eccentricity was cultivated, others say it was natural, still others that his behavior was astonishingly normal for a member of the clerical establishment at the time. In 1744 he published a treatise called *Siris, A Chain of Philosophical Reflections and Inquiries*

Concerning the Virtues of Tar Water. He had become convinced that tar water was a cure for all ills. There was nothing secret or complex about this miracle medicine, which was just what it purported to be: tar and water. There were various recipes for its preparation, but they all came down to the same thing. Some suggested boiling the tar in the water, others involved pounding it. You then let the water stand for several days and simply drank it—presumably throwing away the dregs, unless you wanted black teeth.

Berkeley's treatise on tar water was an immediate best-seller throughout England; people began drinking tar water even in fashionable London coffeehouses. Indigestion, liverishness, gout, "brain fever," the dropsy—all were relieved by this wonder cure, to judge from the grateful letters Berkeley received.

Meanwhile he continued to live the life of an Irish country bishop. In order to help allieviate poverty in the district, he took to wearing clothes produced from local material by the wives of the piggery men and the potato farmers. One contemporary description of his sartorial appearance speaks of "ill clothes and worse wigs." He would enjoy an evening with his cronies when they would "revile the Dutch and admire the King of Sardinia"; and he received a visit from the local Irish giant Cornelius Magrath, who was almost eight feet tall by the time he was fifteen. And then one day Berkeley decided that he'd had enough. He packed up his home and set off with his wife and children for Oxford.

By now it was 1754 and he was almost seventy years old. His physical state had deteriorated to the point where he had to be carried in a horse litter. In Oxford he set up house in Holywell Street with the aim of studying at Christ Church, where his son George was an undergraduate. Berkeley was a tolerant father, and he needed to be: his son had expensive tastes. One day young George arrived at Holywell Street to present his accounts to his father, and announced: "I am ashamed, my lord, to say that I have spent six hundred pounds in six months." Berkeley replied: "Not in vice, I am sure, my child." He then accepted the accounts, checked that they were paid, and consigned them to the fire without further question. (This sum must have involved some prodigious spending, even for those days: it could have bought several race-horses.)

Five months after Berkeley arrived in Oxford, his daughter was reading a sermon to him one winter's night as he lay stretched out on the couch. By the time she had finished he was already cold, his joints stiff. The good bishop was dead.

Recently the new library at Trinity College, Dublin, was named after Berkeley—an apt tribute. In his own time Berkeley had recalled: "the Damps and musty solitudes of the Library [were] without either fire or any thing else to protect Me from the Injuries of the Snow that was constantly driving at the Windows and forcing its Entrance into that wretched mansion." Perhaps it took such conditions to inspire a philosophy that claimed the material world didn't exist—as long as you ignored it.

From Berkeley's Writings

It is evident to any one who takes a survey of the objects of human knowledge, that they are either ideas imprinted on the senses, or else such as are perceived by attending to the passions and operations of the mind, or lastly ideas formed by help of memory and imagination, either compounding, dividing, or barely representing those originally perceived in the aforesaid ways. . . .

But besides all that endless variety of ideas or objects of knowledge, there is likewise something which knows or perceives them, and exercises divers operations, as willing, imagining, remembering about them. This perceiving, active being is what I call *mind, spirit, soul* or *my self.* By which words I do not denote any one of my ideas, but a thing entirely distinct from them, wherein they exist, or, which is the same thing, whereby they are perceived; for the existence of an idea consists in being perceived.

—*A Treatise Concerning the Principles of Human Knowledge*, Part 1, Secs 1, 2

The table I write on, I say, exists, that is, I see and feel it; and if I were out of my study I should say it existed, meaning thereby that if I was in my study I might perceive it, or that some other spirit actually does perceive it. There was an odor, that is, it was smelled; there was a sound, that is to say, it was heard; a color or figure, and it was perceived by sight or touch. That is all that I can understand by these and the like expressions. For as to what is said of the absolute existence of unthinking things without any relation to their being perceived, that seems perfectly unintelligible. Their *esse* is *percipi*, nor is it possible they should have any existence, out of the minds or thinking things which perceive them.

—*A Treatise Concerning the Principles of Human Knowledge*, Part 1, Sec 3

The connexion of ideas does not imply the relation of *cause* and *effect*, but only as a *mark* or *sign* with the *thing signified*. The fire which I see is not the cause of the pain I suffer upon approaching it, but the mark that forewarns me of it. . . . The reason why ideas are formed into machines, that is, artificial and regular combinations, is the same with that for combining letters into words. That a few original ideas may be made to signify a great number of effects and actions, it is necessary they be variously combined together. . . . Hence, it is evident that those things which, under the notion of a cause cooperating or concurring to the production of effects, are altogether inexplicable . . . it is the searching after and endeavouring to understand this Language (if I may so call it) of the Author of Nature, that ought to be the employment of the natural philosopher; and not the pretending to explain things by corporeal cause, which doctrine seems to have too much estranged the minds of men from that Active Principle, that supreme and wise spirit "in whom we live, move and have our being."

—*A Treatise Concerning the Principles of Human Knowledge*, Part 1, Secs 65, 66

Some truths are so near and obvious to the mind, that a man need only open his eyes to see them. Such I take this important one to be, to wit, that all the choir of heaven and furniture of the earth, in a word all those bodies which compose the mighty frame of the world, have not any subsistence without a mind, that their being is to be perceived or known; that consequently so long as they are not actually perceived by me, or do not exist in my mind or that of any other created spirit, they must either have no existence at all, or else subsist in the mind of some eternal spirit: it being perfectly unintelligible and involving all

60

the absurdity of abstraction, to attribute to any single part of them an existence independent of a spirit.

—*A Treatise Concerning the Principles of Human Knowledge*, Part 1, Sec 6

James Boswell's description of Dr. Johnson's famous "refutation" of Berkeley, which evidently seemed equally "near and obvious to the mind" of its demonstrator:

After we came out of the church, we stood talking for some time together of Bishop Berkeley's ingenious sophistry to prove the non-existence of matter, and that every thing in the universe is merely ideal. I observed, that though we are satisfied his doctrine is not true, it is impossible to refute it. I shall never forget the alacrity with which Johnson answered, striking his foot with mighty force against a large stone, till he rebounded from it, "I refute it *thus.*"

—James Boswell, *Life of Johnson*

A more telling criticism from a contemporary of Berkeley, who was more perceptive of the direction in which human thought was evolving:
By giving up the material world, which Berkeley thought might be spared without loss, and even with advantage, he hoped by an impregnable partition to secure the world of spirits. But, alas! the *Treatise of Human Knowledge* wantonly sapped the foundation of this partition, and drowned all in one universal deluge."

—Thomas Reid,
An Inquiry into the Human Mind

Bertrand Russell's modern criticism of Berkeley, referring to Three Dialogues Between Hylas and Philonous:
Philonous says: "Whatever is immediately perceived is an idea: and can any idea exist out of the mind?" This would require a long discussion of the word "idea." If it were held that thought and perception consist of a relation between subject and object, it would be possible to identify the mind with the subject and to maintain that

there is nothing "in" the mind, but only objects "before" it.

—Bertrand Russell,
History of Western Philosophy

John Wheeler, the contemporary U.S. physicist who coined the term "black hole":
No phenomenon is a *real* phenomenon until it is an *observed* phenomenon [his italics].

Chronology of Significant Philosophical Dates

6th C B.C.	The beginning of Western philosophy with Thales of Miletus.
End of 6th C B.C.	Death of Pythagoras.
399 B.C.	Socrates sentenced to death in Athens.
c 387 B.C.	Plato founds the Academy in Athens, the first university.
335 B.C.	Aristotle founds the Lyceum in Athens, a rival school to the Academy.

324 A.D.	Emperor Constantine moves capital of Roman Empire to Byzantium.
400 A.D.	St. Augustine writes his *Confessions*. Philosophy absorbed into Christian theology.
410 A.D.	Sack of Rome by Visigoths heralds opening of Dark Ages.
529 A.D.	Closure of Academy in Athens by Emperor Justinian marks end of Hellenic thought.
Mid-13th C	Thomas Aquinas writes his commentaries on Aristotle. Era of Scholasticism.
1453	Fall of Byzantium to Turks, end of Byzantine Empire.
1492	Columbus reaches America. Renaissance in Florence and revival of interest in Greek learning.
1543	Copernicus publishes *On the Revolution of the Celestial Orbs*, proving mathematically that the earth revolves around the sun.

1633	Galileo forced by church to recant heliocentric theory of the universe.
1641	Descartes publishes his *Meditations*, the start of modern philosophy.
1677	Death of Spinoza allows publication of his *Ethics*.
1687	Newton publishes *Principia*, introducing concept of gravity.
1689	Locke publishes *Essay Concerning Human Understanding*. Start of empiricism.
1710	Berkeley publishes *Principles of Human Knowledge*, advancing empiricism to new extremes.
1716	Death of Leibniz.
1739–1740	Hume publishes *Treatise of Human Nature*, taking empiricism to its logical limits.
1781	Kant, awakened from his "dogmatic slumbers" by Hume, publishes *Critique of Pure Reason*.

	Great era of German metaphysics begins.
1807	Hegel publishes *The Phenomenology of Mind*, high point of German metaphysics.
1818	Schopenhauer publishes *The World as Will and Representation*, introducing Indian philosophy into German metaphysics.
1889	Nietzsche, having declared "God is dead," succumbs to madness in Turin.
1921	Wittgenstein publishes *Tractatus Logico-Philosophicus*, claiming the "final solution" to the problems of philosophy.
1920s	Vienna Circle propounds Logical Positivism.
1927	Heidegger publishes *Being and Time*, heralding split between analytical and Continental philosophy.
1943	Sartre publishes *Being and Nothingness*, advancing

Heidegger's thought and instigating existentialism.

1953   Posthumous publication of Wittgenstein's *Philosophical Investigations*. High era of linguistic analysis.

Chronology of Berkeley's Life

1685   Born March 12 at Dysert Castle, Kilkenny, Ireland.

1696   Goes to Kilkenny College.

1700   Enters Trinity College, Dublin.

1704   Graduates with B.A. degree from Trinity College, Dublin.

1707   Publishes *Arithmetica*. Elected fellow of Trinity College, Dublin.

1709   Publishes *An Essay Towards a New Theory of Vision*, his first major philosophical work.

1710   Ordained as a priest. Publishes first part of *A Treatise Concerning the Principles of*

Human Knowledge, in which he develops his new philosophy.

1713   Publishes *Three Dialogues Between Hylas and Philonous*, which sets out his materialism in literary form. By now he is famous throughout Europe.

1713–1714   Travels to Paris and meets Malebranche just a few days before the French philosopher's death.

1716–1718   Acts as traveling companion to invalid George Ashe on grand tour of Europe.

1724   Leaves Trinity College after twenty-four years to become Dean of Derry.

1728   Marries Anne Forster, a judge's daughter. Sets sail for America, taking up residence at Providence, Rhode Island, while waiting to establish Bermuda college project.

1731   Returns to London after finances

	for Bermuda college are not forthcoming.
1734	Consecrated as Bishop of Cloyne. Publishes *The Analyst; or, a Discourse Addressed to an Infidel Mathematician*, the work in which he attacks the philosophical certainty of mathematics.
1744	Publishes *Siris, A Chain of Philosophical Reflections and Inquiries Concerning the Virtues of Tar Water*, which rapidly becomes a best-seller.
1752	Leaves Ireland and moves to Oxford.
1753	Dies January 14 at Oxford, where he is buried at Christ Church Chapel.

Chronology of Berkeley's Era

1687   Newton publishes *Principia*, proposing universal gravity.

1688   Glorious Revolution deposes Catholic James II. Protestant William of Orange invited from Holland to assume English throne.

1690   Invading forces of James II defeated at Battle of the Boyne, leading to the securing of Ireland by the British.

1703   Death of the diarist Samuel Pepys.

1704	Death of John Locke, founder of empiricism.
1714	James II deposed. George of Hanover invited to become king of England, and ascends the throne to become George I. Death of Louis XIV, the "Sun King," at Versailles.
1715	First Jacobite Rebellion in favor of restitution of Catholic James II.
1716	Death of German philosopher Leibniz.
1720	South Sea Bubble: stock collapse on London market causes heavy financial losses.
1726	Jonathan Swift publishes *Gulliver's Travels*.
1727	Death of Newton.
1732	Birth of George Washington in American colony of Virginia.
1735	Hogarth publishes his series of etchings known as *The Rake's*

Progress, satirizing the life of the period.

1745   Second Jacobite Rebellion, led by Bonnie Prince Charlie, invades from Scotland.

1746   Scottish rebel army slaughtered at Battle of Culloden.

Recommended Reading

George Berkeley, *Three Dialogues Between Hylas and Philonous*, ed. by Robert M. Adams (Hackett, 1979). The philosopher sets out his ideas in Platonic dialogue, making them much more amenable, even if this form may appear to modern tastes somewhat forced.

George Berkeley, *A Treatise Concerning the Principles of Human Knowledge*, ed. Kenneth Winkler (Hackett, 1982). Difficult to read but well worth the effort for those independent spirits who wish to achieve a deeper understanding on their own.

David Berman, *George Berkeley: Idealism and the Man* (Oxford University Press, 1996). The nearest thing to a modern biography now available.

David B. Hausman and Alan Hausman, *Descartes's Legacy: Minds and Meaning in Early Modern Philosophy* (University of Toronto Press, 1997). Places Berkeley's thought in the context of the modern philosophical revolution.

Douglas M. Jesseph, *Berkeley's Philosophy of Mathematics* (University of Chicago Press, 1993). For those who wish to explore further Berkeley's combative ideas on this fascinating topic.

A. A. Luce, *The Life of George Berkeley* (Nelson, 1949). This remains the standard biography, though it is long out of print, and further information has come to light on Berkeley since its publication. Still available in most larger libraries.

Index

A NOTE ON THE AUTHOR

Paul Strathern has lectured in philosophy and mathematics and now lives and writes in London. A Somerset Maugham prize winner, he is also the author of books on history and travel as well as five novels. His articles have appeared in a great many publications, including the *Observer* (London) and the *Irish Times*. His own degree in philosophy was earned at Trinity College, Dublin.